I'm Alive.
I Believe in Everything.

for Linda

I'm Alive. I Believe in Everything.

POEMS NEW AND SELECTED

Lesley Choyce

Breton Books

© 2012 Lesley Choyce

Editor: Ronald Caplan
Production Assistant: Bonnie Thompson
Layout: Fader Communications

The cover painting is by Giuseppe Arcimboldo. Titled "Vertumnus," it was painted 1590-1591 and composed solely of images of fruits, flowers and vegetables. Painted in his native Milan, it is a head-and-shoulders portrait of the Emperor Rudolph II, showing him in the form of the ancient Roman god of vegetation and transformation. In Roman mythology, Vertumnus — also Vortumnus or Vertimnus — is the god of seasons, change and plant growth, as well as gardens and fruit trees. He could change his form at will.

Lesley Choyce on the internet:
http://www.youtube.com/lesleychoyce
http://lesleychoyce.wordpress.com
http://lesleychoyce.blogspot.com
http://www.lesleychoyce.com
http://www.youtube.com/watch?v=IhqAvxueYYU
http://www.youtube.com/watch?v=plN7Jycq9c8

We acknowledge the support of the Canada Council for the Arts for our publishing program.  Canada Council for the Arts   Conseil des Arts du Canada

We also acknowledge support from Cultural Affairs, Nova Scotia Department of Communities, Culture & Heritage. NOVA SCOTIA Communities, Culture and Heritage

We acknowledge the financial support of the Government of Canada through the Canada Book Fund for our publishing activities. Canadä

Library and Archives Canada Cataloguing in Publication

Choyce, Lesley, 1951-
    I'm alive : I believe in everything / Lesley Choyce.
Poems.
ISBN 978-1-926908-17-5
    I. Title.
PS8555.H668I63 2012   C811'.54   C2012-907444-6

Printed in Canada

I'm Alive. I Believe in Everything.

Self. Brotherhood. God. Zeus. Communism.
Capitalism. Buddha. Vinyl records.
Baseball. Ink. Trees. Cures for disease.
Saltwater. Literature. Walking. Waking.
Arguments. Decisions. Ambiguity. Absolutes.
Presence. Absence. Positive and Negative.
Empathy. Apathy. Sympathy and Entropy.
Verbs are necessary. So are nouns.
Empty skies. Dark vacuums of night.
Visions. Revisions. Innocence.
I've seen all the empty spaces yet to be filled.
I've heard all of the sounds that will collect
at the end of the world.
And the silence that follows.

I'm alive. I believe in everything.
I'm alive. I believe in it all.

Waves lapping on the shore.
Skies on fire at sunset.
Old men dancing in the streets.
Paradox and possibility.
Sense and sensibility.
Cold logic and half-truth.
Final steps and first impressions.
Fools and fine intelligence.
Chaos and clean horizons.
Vague notions and concrete certainty.
Optimism in the face of adversity.

I'm alive. I believe in everything.
I'm alive. I believe in it all.

Legend

When I was three years old
and my father was building our house —
nothing there yet but a skeleton of studs
and empty air —
I climbed the ladder to the not-yet attic
and crawled along a joist
just wide enough for infant knees
until I was discovered
in the centre of a would-be home
with mortality singing along my skin
and a cold concrete basement below.

All I had going for me (as usual)
was blind optimism and a sense of balance
like a bright idea not quite lost.
Then, somehow, before the darkness found me out,
my father was aloft,
too scared to shout my name
or make me move.

I think he almost tripped in fear,
a man whose feet could dance through work,
while I just smiled, expecting praise
and found, instead, a painful price
of angry hands that spanked me back
into a world of safe and loved
before the time of further years,
of higher climbs to narrow beams
with legs less sure at every step
and darker depths below us all.

My Father, Shaking Pepper

It was his only vice, I think,
leading to small wars waged at dinnertime.
My mother, silent, all of salt,
would watch his waving wrists with frowns,
his grip around the grey-white glass,
his mind intent on holding ground.

He seemed not sure of when's enough
but peppered plates till seasons flew.
At length, he'd sneeze a stormy gust,
my mother's face spoke: justice done.
She'd cluck her tongue and shake her head;
he'd smile and wipe his glasses clean,
then truces grew around the meal
and love was served its honest share.
So warmed by spices hot as this,
I simply couldn't help but stare.

Saskatoon Bus Depot: 8 a.m. Sunday

The Parktown Hotel's grown sterile in the night;
I slip out to empty streets and something terminal
like this,
the nervous confusion of women in a hall
brooding over hour-long coffee
waiting for home —
for Warham and Longham,
for Biggar and Lanks,
Humboldt and Smeaton,
Carrot River, Nebo, Choiceland,
Cutknife or Livelong.

I'm at home here with the dispossessed —
the bug-eyed lady with her head wrapped
in a white towel,
the hundred-year-old man smiling at his toast,
the grizzled farmer rolling cigarettes with one hand
and the young, chubby sweetheart short-order cook
with eyes cut out from magazines.
I feel community in the sad restaurant
with all the sippers and smokers,
the bare-fisted bacon grabbers
and sports-page sleaze.

Outside the glass, a car stops
and a man who looks like Farley Mowat
refills a bin with *Plain Truth*
while Red Sovine on the radio mewls heartbreak and loss.
All day that country station
will catalogue wasted love and wayward lives
while inside the Saskatoon Bus Depot Restaurant
the Prairies collect in tabled rows,
tea cups steam in October sun
and dreams are swept up with moody brooms.

The settlers here know comfort's short on change,
that waiting's only ever half the size of life

and cities lie to country eyes
more fixed on drying fields of wheat and rye
and winter's meaner passion waiting at home.

My Daughter, With Knots

My six-year-old daughter would come to me
with knots to be untied —
rope and shoelace,
string and sashes.
The mystery behind these knots, at first,
made her angry — but then she grew to understand
there's beauty in the untangling.

The knots once arrived of their own accord but now
she's older and invention is her game —
knots tighter, and more convoluted
than anything nature could conspire on its own.
And still she delivers them to me to
deconstruct,
pretending the work is not her own.
It seems each day, the task is more difficult,
the untangling time grows longer,
the looped geometry more perplexing.
Ten years from now, we'll continue on
at a similar game:
two loose ends, a knot,
a hidden pattern to be followed in
to unravel the core of confusion.

Best Minds

for Allen Ginsberg

I've seen the best minds of my generation
zoned out on Windows
gone Microsoft in the head and lost like cattle
in the perimeters of happiness without a clue
as to the way back home,
who loiter in the shopping malls at lunch hour
pressing thumb and forefinger against
Tommy Hilfiger casual wear,
who can't find spare change from their fashionable pockets
for street musicians or sympathy for bag ladies
collecting Pepsi cans from the garbage.

I've seen the best minds of my generation sitting comatose
in front of *Seinfeld* reruns
secretly admiring George Costanza
and tolerating unimaginable TV commercials
selling garbage for the mind and body,
who finally, frustrated and angry, can only rage
at the remote control
for not being able to make the entire world go mute.

I've seen the best minds browbeaten by bureaucratic barbarism
chained to desks and ergonomic chairs
and losing valuable days of their lives
staring at fax machines and
waiting, waiting for a missive from Montreal or New York
so they can take one step forward or backward
or maybe nowhere at all,
who settle for new Japanese cars with staggering options
instead of freedom from career paths
etched in the ethereal circuitry of the internet
where gigabytes of information wait to pounce
like sleepless lions on the unaware clueless victims
and then drill codework
into the left hemisphere of the brain,
who forgot the lessons of Vietnam and Nixon and Mulroney and Mars

but instead steal away to Club Med to fake euphoria
while frying their pale skin beneath the cancerous sun
while sipping white zombies
and listening to watered down reggae music,
who came home to the city to chow down
at fashionable ethnic restaurants selling artificial foods
instead of homegrown organic fare with lots of fresh herbs
from the garden,
who deal out moments of their lives
like cards in a stacked game of chance,
who arm-wrestle the stock quotations in the *Daily News*,
who stare glassy-eyed at the video lottery machines
in smoky bars at 8 p.m.,
who squelch even harmless daydreams
with easy listening music
or drown themselves in espresso and cappuccino,
who retire from challenges of intellect
for the safety of stadium spectator sports,
who ignore the kids starving in Africa and Asia but wonder
if there's profit in selling soap
and powdered milk to emerging markets,
who sift through junkmail looking for cryptic clues
to the meaning of life as if
the Publishers Clearing House Sweepstakes
has some answer in the fine print,
some respite from the hollowness felt in the bones of loners.

I have seen the best minds of my time
stop trying to react to impossible, intrusive goals
and settle down to dream the dream
of Calvin Klein underwear men and women,
who wake up late at night trying to remember
what crusade it was that sent them shouting in the streets,
who once knew instinctively the Gulf War was never won
but that so many innocent children were killed by their side,
who almost had the courage to say the deficit
was not as important as the destitute,
who almost stood up to the racists and the rich
and the right-wing zealots,

who grew up and trusted the integrity of their banks and senators
and bosses at the corporation
and opted for drinking dark beers from microbreweries as a sign
that they were free-thinking and hip.

They still walk among us and rule and remind their children
that they almost went to Woodstock
and they really did change the world
and they believe in the life force of the planet
and admit that somebody's killing it but
it isn't them.

The best minds still have beating hearts but the blood
fails to find its way to the sleeping brain cells
that store revolution like withered flowers
in the secret place
at the very top of the spinal column.
Yes, I've seen the best of them turn shiny and successful
and boastful of boats and Bay Street, blind with allegiance
to anything but themselves,
lost in a haze of Bacardi ads
and the possibility of retiring early
with the goal of doing nothing
at all but maybe play golf and take naps and wait
for lodging in retirement communities.

Better for them to rage against the glitzy dying of the light
and the tedium of vicarious tabloid living.
Better to froth at the mouth and shout out love
like Milton Acorn in a Toronto park.
Better to recite four-letter words
and get arrested like Ginsberg in San Francisco
or better to sit in the woods alone
and contemplate the sutra of deer tracks
and wintergreen root,
the succulent star moss and sifting mist of spruce trees.

Maybe the problem is that
far too many of us have not gone crazy
but remained sane and stable

and safe within the womb of the twentieth century.

But the howl of young idealism will not go away —
it's there inside your heart;
it's there sneaking up on you at the subway stop;
it's there looking at you from the bubbles in the water cooler
near the photocopier;
it's there in the upper right-hand corner of the picture
of a car wreck on the front page of the paper;
it's there living in your closet with your favourite blue shirt;
it's there, a lost soul in the carburetor of your Lawnboy mower;
it's there in your voicemail like a ghost;
it's there on the other line while you sort out problems
with the Purolator man;
it's sneaking up on you when you least expect it,
reminding you that there's still time,
still time for the best minds of our generation
to give back instead of just taking
because Ginsberg was right when he said,
"Holy the supernatural extra brilliant
intelligent kindness of the soul."

Medicine Walk

When you believe you are beyond repair
let go.
When you cannot be saved by all your friends,
when you cannot be saved by yourself,
forget who you are
and deliver what is left of yourself
to that place
you have been to before
but did not understand its worth.

Use whatever means to get close
but then you must walk the rest of the way
and if you cannot walk
then crawl.
It is your only hope.
The word "sacred" could scare you off
so be silent
be there
and do not ask how
boulders covered with star moss,
wind-bowed apple branches
or the song of a small chanting brook
can salvage you
but they will.

Some very important people I know
have been saved
by the song of the smallest birds;
others redeemed by the smell of leaves rotting in a forest.

Blue Beach

near Hantsport, Nova Scotia

Old dog at the end of the rutted road,
black with a comedy of grey around the mouth
waiting for me to arrive.
She follows me down to the antediluvian shoreline
of Fundy's Minas Basin,
tide sliding out on the smooth flat stones of slate and shale.
Above me, the high graphic cliffs, strata like old books piled
on their sides, some stories more important than the rest.

A black arthritic dog on a black beach
on a warm afternoon, fossils everywhere,
walking back into the Jurassic,
the smell of buried rainforests.
After a morning of rain,
curtains of fresh water fall from mossy slopes above.
Stand behind the cascade,
your back up against the ragged cliff,
and realize how far you've travelled.

Blue Beach — a poet's call
when silted water on black rock
finds that certain slant of light.
My shoes orchestrate a satisfying canticle,
a tempoed crush of thin flat stones.
I help the sea undo these walls of Fundy
as the three of us
hike back into the throat of geography
guided towards the memory
of insects adrift in a tropic rain,
of worms exploring the soft, lavish mud,
of ambitious living things sampling air,
crawling up onto the shoreline
waiting for the twenty-first century.

Black Locusts

I'm thinking of old black locust trees,
wood hard as steel,
alien and deathlike in winter
when icy roads send reckless teenagers
driving their cars into the bark.
Those trees point to the cold moon
like the fingers of old angry men
in private battles with unstoppable pain.

In spring — black trees bloom into white,
a million corsages for the wind,
inside each blossom,
small gifts of seeds for migration's appetite.
In summer, the deep rutted hide of the black locust
is a highway
for earthbound insects to storm the heavens.

The worth of such trees depends on your age.
I'm the thirteen-year-old boy
in the second-storey window,
breathing the perfume of your flowers,
counting the dancers in the ballet of oval leaves
in the sunset
until I find the courage
to call her on the phone
and speak the language
rooted in my heart.

Surfing Before the Hurricane
Nova Scotia, September 1981

South of Sable
the sea busts a gut string,
the wind boils the water mad
and blasts courier waves north
where we greet them armed
with rubber and plastic
at the base of a columned cliff
of dirt that's been shredded
by the Atlantic ever since the glaciers left.

Balanced on such a tiny vessel as this
we paddle like hell
to match the locomotive thrust of the sea
as it tilts up at the sky
ignoring the repressions of gravity and stasis.

The wind pumping off the land like a handshake
ripples up the chest of this monster
as I feel my bloodless hands dig deeper
then I'm dropping down the front
a satisfied suicide in an elevator shaft
my only contact with the sea
a square inch of fin that slices
like a razor down the watery ribcage.

Up ahead, the machinations of water and wind
conspire a cold green blast furnace
a cylindrical chamber of beauty and terror
the last thundering echo
of the message from three hundred miles out.

First fading dangerously back into the throat
then driving recklessly across
this screaming wall
I write my own brief graffitti
of praise

and in the end lose the bid for an exit
as the tube collapses all around,
a shuddering mass of mangled sea
that drives me like a spike
to the bottom
where my puny flesh is twisted and thrashed
until I surface unrestricted again
into the blazing world
of oxygen and blue sky.

The Dragonfly Inside the Wave

All I can really do
is report
what I saw.
On a sunny blue day in August,
paddling my board seaward
past heaven-hollowed North Atlantic waves,
here comes this giant dragonfly
flying hell-bent out of the tube
and straight up into the heavens
as if he's done it
a thousand times before.

Trepidation

I know all about fear:
fear is the hand that holds me down
when the broken wave
swarms over me with cold December's churning sea
as it coils around my head
and wraps my legs with baling wire
and only my arms flap free like strange frantic birds.

Fear is the hand that shakes with death
and greets the deep
that wants my bones.
So often lately, you seek me out
and probably you know the trick
to turn the mind and almost win.
But when I'm sucked beneath the wave
and surface only next to find
another larger, meaner foe
I ply my trade of quiet grief
and swim direct into the throat
of smashing seas and cold regret,
then dive to depths
where calm collects
and anchors hope with simple dreams.

By then when my lungs are near collapsed
and dread has gripped my neck at last
I call forth hope to swim me up
while fear gives up and hurries home
its name inscribed inside my skull,
its thumbprint blue upon my throat.

The Necropolis, Glasgow

Old dead rich men buried here
above the modern brewery
that bathes the city with a yeasty smell,
the occasional burst of burnt malt
conspired by a workman angry at his boss.

These graves have seen the work of diggers in the night
stealing fresh corpses for the school of medicine one year,
searching out rings and necklaces
from the elegant fermented dead
on other occasions.

The pubs of Glasgow saw many men
conspire through the centuries
over dark beers
where and when to dig,
return later for a second draught
as the moon rose higher in the night
to lift a pint to health,
another to the thing that steals it away
and allows a poor man a living.
Soiled hands around an amber glass,
as the sweet sickly smell of a coal fire
reminds him of one comforting thought.
He who dies of wealth is as dead as he who dies of dearth,
the only difference this:
the poor have better guarantees
to stay undisturbed
in the thin, cold soil of this bonnie land.

December Day at Little Gidding

An old man with a wheelbarrow
refusing to offer up directions without full theatre;
before he mentions a left-hand turn by the hedge,
he's twelve and on his first
horse on a green pasture
with his mother fearing for his safety and him
hanging on for dear life.

As if to illustrate some consummate point,
he picks up his hoe
and holds it up with two strong brown hands.
"It was down that way; at least it was when I was a boy."
Like a literate fool, I ask if that's the place,
the small retreat, the chapel, the poem from *Four Quartets* by Eliot.
"Don't know no Eliot. Perhaps there was once.
And a chapel, yes.
Strong religion in that place.
I never believed in God till one Sunday
in there with the light through the stained glass
shining down on the ankle of a girl
along the pew.
Heaven took me then
and never gave me back."

The Death of Donut Land and Other News

Sad history here in the gypsum hills of Hants —
the new Tim Hortons off the 101
has slain Donut Land.
The clones continue to kill off all of us
who are one of a kind.
The aged and tilting chimney of the old textile mill in Windsor
so Italian in its angle against the summer sky
has been razed for safety sake and in its place
a single polished metal pipe
set vertical like an insult to gravity and tradition.
I share the grief of ten thousand swallows.

A meeting with fairy-tale actors in the attic of an old school
surrounded by a troupe of life-size puppets
some more real, more interesting, than the people I meet elsewhere.
Several join us for lunch at the vegetarian café
and order nothing more
than soup du jour and toast, a cup of Grimm
with a twist of lemon.

I drive back out of the birthplace of hockey
turn left to a dead end down Old Irishman's Road
retrace my track to Sweet's Corner
a bridge on the St. Croix River
where I can abandon civilization altogether
wade through chest-high sweet summer dykeland grass
descended from the seeds of the Acadians
swept away in the higher tides of Europe's stubborn wars.

The soft stone beneath the grass breeds karst sinkholes
known to grow hungry and swallow Jersey cows.
I step lightly here and hold my arms straight out.
From the road I look like a city fool
pretending he's an airplane
or a clown singing opera in an open field.
I trust the air but not the ground

and at every fifth step feel something like a six-volt thrill of pain
the sting of purple thistle invisible in the timothy.

On the hottest afternoon of the year, I climb the high white cliffs
that crumble like stale bread each time I step
use tree roots for handholds and railings
and pull myself up into the cool shade of the forest
whose floor is cratered from the karst
small dark canyons filling with generations
of pine cones.

Two miles along the escarpment in a sweltering heat
then down to feel the suck of Fundy wind in the estuary
and a tidal field of salt hay
flat and neatly combed by a falling tide
the beautiful hair of all the women on earth.

When the wind stops dead, mosquitoes and blackflies
take license to test my sanity.
I fail all the tests, retreat, sprint over cracked glazed mud
curling up into half-formed bowls
jump three snaking brown streams
until
a thunderhead appears to the north
as one bull thistle draws fresh blood from my calf
urging me to climb a blue-white gypsum hillside
hunker on a bluff
cradling myself in the roots of a massive pine
my fingers tucked deep into the history of the bark
as thunder fills the valley
slides its broad vernacular into every crevice in these tumbling hills
and fills my head
with wonder.

A Love of Old Things

There is a love for old things.
Even when they break
they can be fixed
almost always a sense
of wonder built into the basics
of their necessity.

New things are formed
without pretence of a soul
and when they fail
must be replaced
with something even newer.

I am not ashamed
of the sills rotting in my old house
and like a good surgeon
I remove the part of a beam
that has served well
for nearly two centuries.
I carve younger wood
to embrace the old
and foster kinship with ten-inch nails.
There is kindness
in the swing of the hammer
its hard-headed kiss
even though the sound of metal hitting home
scares the pigeons from the eaves.

Time itself is an old thing
and heals itself
if you are willing to help.
The past we repair
over and over
but today is thrown away
with the false expectation that tomorrow
will replace it with something
better.

Song of Myself
for Walt Whitman

My song is speech
a chorus of life's culled glossary
for voice to celebrate
all that is.
Far beyond the threads of sinew
that string my words together
there are arms and legs
and sometimes a sensible brain.
I am confused like you and make
a small religion of my dilemma;
I am proud, like you are, over
small victories of making it through
a bad afternoon.

No one but me (and you, of course) is so great
at lamenting one's own diminished deeds
until it all turns into a work of art
as everything should.

I'm drawn into every flame
even the holocaust
but pull back when my eyebrows singe.
I assume, as you assume,
we are all more and less than what appears
but we grow great temperament at green moments:
at the crosswalk standing
with an old woman in a shawl
who knows you;
or at sunrise, standing on
leaves of grass
wearing perfect shrouds of ice.

Orion Keeps Me Honest

Orion keeps me honest —
the old hunter with the squared shoulders
keeps track of how true I am to myself.
He's lost, at times, on the coldest nights
when the north wind conjures up the camouflage
of the great milky wash of stars
but usually Orion stares down
at me
when I forget just where I am
or why.
My daughter, at three, renamed the hunter
O'Brien
and refused to believe he ever killed anything,
Greek or Irish, of this earth or in the sky.
If constellations have souls
then Orion's is large, expansive and light —
and he's a vegetarian like me.
We know there are many different breeds of warriors.
Some find kindness to be a worthy grenade
against every foe.
The sky is filled with every sort:
some stars point us north or south
some scramble east to west.
These days Orion seems to be content
to station there
beyond my back door
and when he sees us emerge
on a frozen night —
pretends we are something immortal
speaks caution to the wind
and spreads the rumour to all the other gods
in the neighbourhood.

Testament

I give you the square root of sky,
the large province of hope
and the view from
the top of the hill at the end of the beach.
I give you finches in the apple tree
and the sunset, west over ice,
the wedge of sunlight in late afternoon
with its warm explosion of colour
at the end of a dark day —
the brooding clouds still overhead,
unable to repress the adventure.

I give you every beautiful thing
that ever washed up on our shore —
the remains of glass bottles
sculpted into gems
left lying in the sand on a spring morning.
I give you all lost toys
and the right to re-invent
all worlds to fit your dreams.
I give you newborn birds in your cupped hands
and the resurrection of small wild creatures.
I give you back all that knowledge and
responsibility have taken away
and so I set you free.

I give you a room full of balloons
and I also give you balance —
the ability to walk with assurance
calmly along any precipice and never look down.
I give you solid footing with each and every step
and guardians
in the form of wind and snow
and foam from the sea.

I give you the compass from my desk
and the map I've kept hidden in my heart —

the tools to find the path from despair to happiness
and I will show you how to use them well
and finally this:
the warm wind in your face
as you ride a wild Appaloosa
across a field of clover and Queen Anne's lace —
the solved mystery of being and moving
at once.

All the Water in the World

April 1, 2003

I am thinking about all the water in the world,
how it moves itself around day after day
in its own adventures.
Below my office, after the spring rains,
it is creeping up to the perimeter of my garden.
The wide marsh expected this
and drowns itself with the luxury
of rising tides,
mixing winter's sea with melting ice.

Elsewhere in the province, bridges tumble,
roads collapse and houses silt up
(a kitchen has a riverbed for a floor).

No one is dying or anything
just rain having its way with your stalled car in traffic,
leaking chimneys, water blowing up under your eaves.

The two ducks are back
in the flooded pools:
one perfect dark pair
returning every year
to this sacred place
beyond my wind-sculpted apple trees,
the same two ducks, it seems
who love to watch me plant
and weed.

Half of my land is below sea level today
awash in the way that water cleanses
while white plumes of waves at sea
leap up into the atmosphere
spending the final fury of yesterday's storm
throwing foamy spray at the clouds
like confetti at a wedding.

The tears have fallen, pelted down
on yesterday's windshield —
wipers unable to keep up.

The storms pass quickly now and congratulate themselves,
not like when I was a boy
and dreary rain would intimidate me for days,
grinding me down.
Now it's one solid slap and it's over,
the geese applauding at sunset
while all the water in the world
settles itself back down
into the deep democracy of itself.

Writing Down the Wind

I remember everything the morning said
a reminder that
the first poem I spoke
was a gasp of air
borrowed from a hurricane
the same breeze still blowing through me
fifty years later
always fresh
inhalation, recollection
exhalation, recognition
that the torrent in my throat
is something borrowed.

Like you I have swallowed clouds and skies
while running to catch the sunset
as a child
panting hard to save what was left of the day
as the darkness swallowed up
the town behind me.

Having learned the several occupations
of pain, sorrow, recovery, healing
I use the best of each to forge a language
capable of translating the optimism of trees
like those ragged white pines, higher than the rest
scribes of the seasons
who spend their days
writing down the wind.

Hauling Seaweed for My Garden

I feel like I have discovered gold
sailed my Ford station wagon
down the road on my attenuated quest
until there upon the shore
heaps of it
raw and lovely, dark in wealth.

Some thrill, some grand satisfaction
hums through the symphony of my bones
as I wield the three-pronged pitchfork
and thrust riches into buckets and bins.

Rotting already and jumping with bugs
the dulse, Irish moss, sea lettuce
and even the corpuscular kelp
is collected, compacted
settled into the back of my car.

Head spinning with my success
I sail back home down the asphalt channel
to my queen
the unturned garden of spring
her dark skin still tinged with a rime of frost
her womb still haunted by the solemnity of winter
and I lavish these gifts upon her
while the leafless wisteria
and muted rhododendron
try to hide their happiness.

This Poem is the Room

This poem is the room you were in
when you heard about her death.
The poem has four walls and you are there
holding a telephone in one hand
and the rest of your life in the other.
The room has changed because of the news
and the photograph of her holding you
grows larger
and the windows don't seem to work as well.
They begrudge the light.
A clock is ticking although the room
wants to stop it and stretch out the seconds.
There are meaningless shelves of books
that once were worth reading.
This is a room where you wrote to her
spilling the heaviness in your heart.
The letter was not sent
but of course the room remembers
everything.
After the phone call, you sit down
in the room and it swallows up
everything around you
as it becomes a poem,
shedding dimension in order to
accommodate
the dark luxury of all you remember.

Report from the Republic of Morning

The votes are counted:
all things alive are in favour of spring.
The small commonwealth of birds —
gull, raven, eider, loon, shearwater,
impulsive swallow, dropping from the clouds,
first lonely heron poking at the mirrored pool,
all approve.

On the trail behind the headland,
smell of morning musk of last night's fox,
crunch of gravel beneath these old, notorious shoes
on what was once a gypsum railway
now a path for solitary dreamers,
escapees from the usual tyranny of escalating obligation,
reminding themselves that everything on a morning like this
is the opposite of trivial.

Before the sea wind rises, the sparrow's song rules,
the skilful anthem large, symphonic,
soundtrack for the ballet of mist
over the dark Lawrencetown River
flooded with the ambition of wet gravity and moons.

Everything speaks of promise here,
the crowded blue mussels in the clear water,
the first pale shoots of spruce,
the green and ancient horsetails
glazed with melting frost.

On the bridge, the water racing beneath,
as good a place as any
to stir the options: east or west,
civilization or its opposite.
A quick ballot and the decision stands.
Turn back east towards the rising sun
and seek the counsel
of sand and sea oats and all the sage advice
left by the slipping tide.

The Sophistication of Pencils

I have not written a poem with a pencil
for nearly ten years
and now this —
such a surprise of sound
the hissing of lead, the volume of it all.
I hadn't realized how silent pens are
and how much more muscle it takes
to bear down on the lead
to force it to make sense.

Erasers on pencils, of course
haven't worked properly since
sometime in the previous century
so I won't even go into that.
Already I am nostalgic for the soft rubber perfection
of the erasers of my youth
all gone now.
But back then
well, you made a mistake
you fixed it right away.
Now, just a smudge and a curse.

The pencil poem should be long and thin
I think
and have a shiny band of metal
but the older I get
the fatter the poems
my desperation calling out to the language
to be generous, to set out a buffet
of so many good things.

I'm sure there was a boy once
with clumsy crayon fingers
who craved the use of a pencil
saw his mother with the *Post*
attending to the religion of crossword puzzles
and his father, with one in his fist

sitting with his tea in a pool of kitchen table light
arranging the family's fortune with numbers on a page
a spare one mounted over an ear
like a missile at ready
if he needed reinforcements.
I'm sure the boy heard the hissing, scratching sound
and craved the sophistication of pencils
could not wait to give up his grasp
on those thick bright colours
and take on the important work
of reducing the world
to black and white.

Poem for Leander's Garage

There is wisdom here and wrenches
a calendar by the window
of a long retired month
with a photo of a woman smiling at new tools.
Her planet is one that is clean and shining
while here, in this world
everything is broken and needs fixing.

Leander has my car on a lift
and the ice melts from it
to create a soft dirty rain falling to the floor.
Whatever is wrong with my car
must be bad
because Leander mutters only one syllable or two.
I can't hear him anyway
with the damn compressor
hammering all the silence out of the afternoon.
It's warm inside at least
with the oil drum wood stove at work
chewing up the logs of spruce
with boisterous flames.

Someone has recorded history
all over the sweating floor
using the language of automobiles:
a ruined transmission for a war,
a stripped engine block, a difficult battle,
worn-out tires like the death of senators,
brake pads and discs
ground down by someone trying to slow down the future.

The clamps and bolts are parts of speech
long forgotten
but trails of automotive fluids string it
all together as if the narrative makes sense.
When the compressor motor stops

all that is left is the snapping and hissing of the stove spruce.
Snow sifts in like desert sand
under the garage door.

Leander admits he found something that
doesn't look too good
but it can probably be repaired.
He walks out from under the pavilion of my flawed car
and wipes his hands on an oily rag,
doesn't pronounce the verdict
until we've had a chance
to discuss politics
and old philosophy
and the fact that
he and I are a day older than yesterday,
lucky, damn lucky, the pair of us.
He sips cold, brown coffee
from a smudged Tim Hortons cup
and waits for me to say
something equally profound.

Driving North With the Dalai Lama

The car's engine thrums to
his voice on a recording
as the highway collects the province
on both sides
sets it behind us and funnels us on
to the Bay of Fundy.

Alone in a car with a holy man
is a fine place
to consider his crazy brilliance:
that we must pity
the rich and famous
because they cannot remain
one or the other
so our compassion is needed.

The bare trees beside the road
only days from finding spring
make a small salute to time:
suffering now, or suffering in the future
is pretty much the same.

Small crosses and stuffed animals appear beside the road
and the despair of some stranger's past
arrives like a clever hitchhiker
and clears space in the front seat
waits for my tears
and steadies the wheel
as the world goes out of focus.

The Buddhists have this other point of view
the Dalai Lama says
impressed as much as I am
with the fine view of Cape Blomidon
and the tableau of pruned orchards
in the foreground —
another way to look at compassion.

We have all lived many lives, he reminds us
millions perhaps
in this and other worlds
(although he is vague as to which ones)
perhaps infinite lives
(now I wonder if he's grandstanding — carried away
by the wings of his profundity).
And?
And one must realize that each person that you meet
was once your mother in a previous existence.
So you would not want to be unkind to your mother —
she protected you when you were so young.

I stop to stretch a tight knee and walk into the forest
a thrush for an audience, mayflowers proclaiming everlasting life,
a river pouring all its enthusiasm into a deep pool.
George W. Bush was once my mother, I now must surmise
and Henry Kissinger. Charles Manson.
Idi Amin. Richard Nixon.
And what other felons and tyrants have I myself
given birth to and loved?
The warm air of this Annapolis Valley
feels heavy in my throat
the towering elm trees, all dead
still hold their massive arms aloft
to shoulder the sky.

All forms of suffering seem to be gone when I return to my car
as the Dalai Lama waits in silence.
He is in no hurry
with all the time in this world and the next ones available.
Standing by the side of the road
I wait for the sparrows to sing to me
from the top of the tamarack tree
which is collecting the sunlight madly
like a wild beggar
astonished at the sudden generosity
of the world.

The Language of Broken Things

My glasses for example
are taped on one corner but work well.
They cannot travel in my pocket since they do not fold
but some of us are like that
and still useful.

Most pens I find around the house
(when I'm frantic for one,
full blooded with a notion to jot down)
most pens are capless, chewed or drying out.
My great hope the ink will last for one
more poem
but I'm willing to use it
to just scratch on the page if I have to
and translate it later
rubbing charcoal on the surface
as if it were an old tombstone.

My garden shed is full of half-handled shovels and rakes
two-tined pitchforks and a clutter of parts.
My closet is a museum of shorted-out toasters
raspy radios without knobs
leaky faucets saved for parts
and a half-forgotten baseball glove of rotting leather.

The trash men will never drive off with this version of my life.
I'm saving everything for possible use.
All the broken, nearly useless things speak to me
like cousins from my childhood
begging me to put them to use.
Very few whine and feel sorrow
over the loss of their shiny origins.
There is pride in broken things
lost in drawers or cocooned in basements
or asleep in the attic
where the sunlight sneaks in through the cracks

under the eaves above them
to illuminate the tips of roofing nails
wearing perfect jackets of frost.

The Discipline of Ice

I am once again falling in love with this land. Myself, crumpled son of January snow, shoveller of driveways, toqued against the gentle onslaught falling from above, snowplow arriving early, dog barking at my neighbour. We are all waking up and greeting the new white land.

On the radio I hear that Peter Gzowski is dead. This burns a hole in my morning map of Canada. A cigarette burning down the town of Upper Rubber Boot, Saskatchewan. Gone. I'm still threading it all together in this trick of tethering, working the proper knots for holding down geography, meadows, drumlins, and superior lakes.

I remember my own morning over Mutton Bay, Lower North Shore of Quebec. The helicopter landing me on a platform of four good sheets of plywood set up in a backyard and covered in ice. Spring just around the corner in May. Men in sheds building boats made from trees skidded out of the woods by horses, me spending an evening talking with the young wife of the town's minister, away that night forty miles north by skidoo for a funeral.

On another occasion, driving to Lloydminster, Saskatchewan in the worst rental car ever — ten years old in bad condition, the company going out of business next week anyway. But a proper car for a poet on the Yellowhead Highway following the raven tracks to the Alberta border. The reading was a classic no-show event, audience all at the ice rink or watching American midget wrestlers in town for one night only. Muffler falls off on the way back to Saskatoon and a one-armed mechanic at the truck stop welds it back together, cigarette dangling from his mouth, the CBC rasping from the wall radio that hasn't been turned off since the sixties because the switch won't work.

Twenty-five years into this relationship and I'm still in love with the new country, my chimney in bad repair, my lungs not what they used to be. The seawater on my face in winter seems colder now than when I was young and didn't care. Now, I care and confront, signed a big contract with caution to work on my behalf.

There was the year the ice came in and we walked to sea, island by island — blue sky above these chunks of the St. Lawrence flushed to sea, wind driven south and then back to land like an invading army of ice on the beach. Big blocks of blue-white bergs as far as the horizon allows. Step by step off the continent and beyond until the wind shifts and a mad scramble to race ashore, leaping to a flat pan that cracks in half. Next one tilts up on end when I come tumbling out of the sky onto its edge. Back on shore, a crowd of us watching the islands depart, sliding south to their melt, our tongues still frozen in our mouths. Big spring boots filled with seawater from the final almost-successful leap to shore.

A warm September morning while I build on to my house, bag of nails on a wood floor, spruce boards, raftering in the sky, climbing up and down the morning ladders, ladder-legged by eleven, craving coffee, Murray McLauchlan on the CBC pining for Gzowski, his voice full of praise and pity this day with me hammering lumber in place to hold up a roof willing to support snow two feet deep — uncertain as always that I know what I'm doing but doing it anyway. Making up rules as I hammer on, then starting to sing something I heard or made up in my head. Geese decide to fly overhead and I have a feeling that there will be waves by afternoon. A light breeze out of the north predicts a great yearning for the past, the one I'm hammering into place this very minute beneath the sky of the new land.

In the next glacial age the stones will sing our anthems to the cold and dark until the politics of planets sets the sun's fire again to soothe the discipline of ice.

This Poem

Somebody once told me to get angry in a poem
so this poem is angry.
This poem is so angry
it wants to give me a kidney punch
and throw me out into the snow
because this poem has been waiting around
for a long time to be written
and it's mad as hell.
So I have to be apologetic to this poem
and invite it in for a cup of coffee
but it's hard to quiet this poem down,
so I'll let it speak its piece first.

You can hear this poem shouting
on an empty street at dawn,
scratching its fingernails on a trash can
and breaking empty bottles,
calling the whole world crazy
but I hear police sirens
so I'm gonna tell this poem to go hide
in a snowbank and pretend it's asleep.

But now this poem is going to have to wake up
because somebody else told me
that a poem should have an important message.
So my poem is carrying around protest signs
up and down in front of laboratories
and ice floes and missile silos.
This poem is against dark altogether
but isn't convinced light is the answer.
This poem, in fact, knows what happens
when we die
but it's keeping its mouth shut about that.
This poem isn't stupid.

This poem has prairie train whistles
on tape loops inside its ears

and has X-ray vision to see into homes at night
where it gets real lonely.
It's just a rusted-out heart, this poem.
It's just bleeding metal everywhere
because this poem is not stainless steel.
I see it getting down on all fours and this poem
has become so low
it has to eat breakfast underneath abandoned refrigerators.
It sleeps inside carpet underlay.
This poem's best friend is gravity
and it sings itself to sleep
in octaves only used for defense purposes.

I still keep trying to tell this poem to get serious,
to wear glasses and a tie,
to say something profound
like all those other poems.
But this poem is tired of being pushed around.
It doesn't trust me any more.
It refuses to be serious and right now
it's holding a raffle on eternity,
it's playing clarinet with its toes
and dreaming us all into oblivion.
It hopes to run for president soon
because that's where all the comedians are.
It wants to set up a shoeshine parlour in the Oval Office
and charge five cents a shine.
This poem wants to dismantle all the generals
back to random bones
and sing Chuck Berry songs
in all the White House bathrooms at night.
This poem didn't know it would get so political.

And now, this poem
wants to look you straight in the eye
and be part of your soul.
It wants to know the colour of your underwear
and your blood type.
It wants to be there watching the brand

of laundry detergent you buy.
This is a very baffled poem.
It doesn't understand, for example,
why nobody ever told me to write a poem about happiness.
This poem would like to be
as happy as a kid with a pitcher of Kool-Aid.
It would like to be a hummingbird, maybe,
or a hippopotamus with some great mud.
This poem can't find happiness
anywhere in its concordance.
Its gonna have to keep on going
until it finds it
even if it has to speed up
and continue on for 5,550 years.
This poem wants to be read
at the speed of light.

The Man Who Borrowed the Bay of Fundy

In a hospital bed in Mississauga,
on fire with a disease
that has travelled too far
through the inland channels of his blood,
he stares hard at the white wall
and squeezes the years together,
looks through the lifting mist
and glazed red mud,
knowing that any minute now
the bore will come racing in,
the boats will wobble left and right
and in no time,
the tide will be licking at the grass line again
as if it had never left,
as if nothing had changed at all.

The White Wheelbarrow

The world has gone wrong today,
the sky hangs low with clouds like threats.
Insects close in for the kill
or wait behind glass
for tragedy and panic.

And then the back door barks open —
my daughter is bored;
she's found an ancient rusted can
of paint
and claims dominion.
We pry it open to find
an immaculate velvet cloud of creamy white,
still liquid beneath the skin.
She sees the thrill in all that innocence
and wants a chance to change the world.

I find a brush, a prayer, a rolling frame
of overworked machine
to set before a saviour
and now I'm sitting back upon the porch,
as my daughter paints the wheelbarrow white.
Across the lake the sky unlocks with loud reports
but the wind is on our side
and now I see just how
so much depends.

The Beautiful Thing About My Outhouse

The beautiful thing about my outhouse
is that it's tucked away
beside a gnarled broken-down and resurrected
crabapple tree
where goldfinches dance at arm's length
not believing I'm inside
with the door open.
This place is surrounded by jewelweed
stapled to the outside walls
and leaning through the doorway
selling those miniature orange orchids.
The hummingbirds fly here
from South America
just to park in orbit
in front of this place
while inside
I collect the sound of their wings
so I can play it back in winter
when the cold makes my breathing go short.

And the beautiful thing about my outhouse
is that it's still here
after all the fallen-down years;
it's forgotten by everyone but me.
The wood is bleached and rotting,
harmonizing its way back into the rich soil.
Ants drill out the sills,
leave little cones of sawdust
like literature on the floorboards.
It leans west towards sunset
and I've propped the south wall
against gravity and soft footings
while a jungle of wild roses
blooms in summer
and grows long powerful arms

that embrace this holy place
and keep it upright.

The beautiful thing about my outhouse
is the way a single, pale raspberry root
slides its way overnight
through the spruce floor
and makes straight for the roof,
tendrils curling out around the beams
pushing a tiger head of green
that finds a knothole up high
and immigrates toward light.

The deer don't believe my outhouse exists.
They wander like lost cattle around the berries
and scratch along the cornerposts.
My neighbours all think it hasn't been used for years
and if the government knew
I'd have to tear it down.

The beautiful thing about my outhouse
is that it's so old and persistent
it has become a living thing rooted in the planet
and can't be destroyed.
It's true, a drunk neighbour
once peppered the door with birdshot
but the outhouse was empty.
The holes make good ventilation and with the door closed
the sun projects a crazy constellation.
The only violence here is the chorus of mosquitoes
who arrive at dusk
looking for the blood of the distracted.

Forest Fire on the Eastern Shore

In a hotel in Yellowknife I learn that a forest fire
is about to sweep away my home
back on the coast of Nova Scotia.
It seems a sad betrayal of some plot
that has worked so well for so long for me.

No way to fly there in time to beat away the flames
so I turn on the CBC
and watch a fire that is so angry and bold,
it mimics my own unrest these recent months.

My old house calls out to me from across the weary continent.
It says, I know things have been rough
but I won't let you down.
It has already read my mind and knows
I'm thinking I may have nothing to return to.

I watch the merciless hooligan flames encouraged by a heady wind
licking the blue sky as they devour the helpless thin spruce
and torch the unsuspecting ferns and alders.
I turn off the TV and the old house reminds me
that some things never die.
Some things have a habit of going on and on
even if grey ash is all the evidence remaining,
but it also assures me that will not happen now
even though the firefighters are losing ground
and only the sea will stop
the scorching parade.

I fall asleep to the sound of a TV hockey game
in the next room
and, in the rarest of gestures,
shake hands with fate.
In the morning I learn
that water bombers from Newfoundland
have arrived
with a cargo of hope.

A month later, walking the scorched terrain
I sift through the black ash
to find pale new shoots of optimism
and smudge my cheeks as ceremony,
reminding myself
to always believe
in the religion
of green.

Paint-By-Number Garden of Gethsemane

Christ sat sadly on his rock waiting for a child
to give him colour — make him human.
They were marketing this genuine Paint-By-Number
sad moment in the Woolco store. It was Sunday
and my father had taken me there to buy tires.

"You gotta have good tires," he told me,
trying to save me from destruction.
(I wanted to install some weathered beauties I had
resurrected from a used tire graveyard. There
had been a 6.50/15, two 7.25/15s and even an
F70 which I had to roll a big rock off of to get.)

But when my father-being-a-truck-mechanic-for-all-his-life
looked at them, he said, "This is junk. These tires
are no good. Look at the nail holes in this one."

So he bought me some new tires — new black ones,
not even recaps.
I felt bad, being twenty-three years of age and unable
to afford a new set of tires. (But I do have a
woman, a goat, a Volkswagen bus and 9/10 of a
master's degree in English.)

I had tried putting my 9/10 master's degree in English
on my wheels, using the Romantic Period as a
guide. But they went flat right off.

That's when I went to the tire graveyard and
eventually the Woolco Gethsemane.

Walking out of the store with a tire over
each of my shoulders, the bereft saviour
looked so pale and unforgiving
despite the fact that the garden was filled with
his colourless disciples, the numbers 1 to
168, all waiting for paint
to make them real.

The Possible Ear of God

When I was a child
I thought like a child,
I sang into the cement mixer like a child.
I thought that singing into the cement mixer
Made me sound like
Nat King Cole
Or Bing Crosby.
This was the same cement mixer my father was using
To build our house:
One part Portland Cement
Three parts sand
Four parts my father.
My father's only song in the cement mixer
Was the gravelly grumble of the
Cement mixing
The staccato of the shovel clanking
On the revolving cylinder
The melody of the hose
Washing out the sludge.
At the end of the day
After a wall was finished
Soon after the six o'clock supper
I stalked back to the work site
And sang my songs into the cement mixer.

I braced my hands on the still hose-wet rim
Feeling the pleasant damp cold
And I made that machine work overtime
Using my voice not motor
To make the music hall orbit
Mixing and remixing my singing
Inside this
The possible ear of God.

Tom Gilbert's Pants

He's dead now.
We live in his old house.
The wooden beams in the basement sag.
They accentuate the curve
of Tom's old baggy pants
looped between two nails in the attic.
Tom hung them there once
after coming home from ship —
"Ninety hours from Halifax to Boston," he'd say,
bragging.
But now the pants, the beams,
sagging.

Old Tom, dead
(lived his last years somewhere else with a bitchy
woman who took him in, got the money from his house).
The house stood empty.
The hunters came
blew out the windows,
buckshot miraculously ending up in a pocket
of Tom's pants,
along with ancient tobacco and a tiny pipe
fashioned from a bottle cap and a hollow stick.

The day I bought the house from Tom and his keeper,
he sagged all over,
his pants barely lashed to his pencil-thin waist,
his erector-set shoulders barely bolted on.
And when he went to sign his name
the words sloped downward,
below the line
toward the basement of the page.

40-Watt Lighthouse

It's frigidly late at night.
I'm driving home across the winter-stripped marsh,
my headlights fading like sick yellow flowers.
The sea heaps up on the right
lacing the air with salted ice,
rusting away my automobile
even now as I make for home
on the stone-strewn highway.

Somewhere in this uncharted wildness
my house clings to the shale hill,
a bare 40-watt bulb endorses the porch,
pays lip-service to the night.

Eye on that essential beacon,
I flail my ailing beast homeward
through the storm.
The sweat freezes my hands to the wheel
and we are locked
into the only way home
as the night, the wind, the sea,
conspire to make me believe
I can never make it.

Modern Translations

She is impossibly old, we all know that.
Her hands dance in the air,
creating invisible calligraphy
in a language time itself
cannot translate.

Her speech is mostly gone,
the sound of words has evaporated
over the years,
has gone up towards the sky
but she can still move her mouth
while her hands dance.

She grew up in Italy
in the province of Abruzzi ,
where I know she danced in the hills,
a beautiful young girl
still dancing behind the toothless
grin and a chinful of
stubble that, if I was ten years
younger and it was mine,
I would have bragged about.
I was taught how to say
the word *strawberries* in Italian;
when she hears me
sing it in her ear,
she closes her eyes
and blushes.
We are on the hills of Abruzzi
unlocking the world with our tongues;
she remembers
who I am.

The Bill Tawger School of Etiquette

Dipping one galvanized bucket
at the end of a pole
into the well
(nearly dry, a long dip down) to water the cows.
The fog hovers off the coast, just barely offstage.
I ride my bike with no brakes by old Bill as he dips
in agony, some sort of private hell
that forever excludes even the luxury of a hand pump.

Stubborn as a rusted bolt, old Bill, tongue locked
in cheek, one eye squinting at the disappearing sun,
pants like angular army tents barely held up
by a busted suspender.
For the fifteenth time I yell hello to
the old fart
and he never breaks stride in the dip,
just sort of grunts like he's got better to do
than waste a breath.
Then his favourite cow knocks the bucket off the pole
so Bill claps her on the ear
and yells off into the waiting fog a curse
at the bastard who made his life
so damn difficult.

All Alone and Lost in the Northwest Territories

Not quite summer yet
and the tornado of blackflies swirls just above my head.
Here I sit on a bald slab of rock,
pale and stunned beneath the sun
in a wilderness so vast
it cannot be imagined
by the small geography of my mind.

The trail was poorly marked
but this overconfident poet
believed he could
remember his way back,
forgetting that memory itself
is an empire of false paths
and deceptive maps.

And now this:
good and truly lost
and no one to save me but me.
The stubborn repetition of the landscape is no help.
The stunted trees, the bare swatches of stone all look the same
as the curious raven eyes me from his privileged perch.

This eastern hiker has been lost before
in familiar Nova Scotia woods
but there is no place in such a province where
a mortal is ever more than thirty miles from the sea
and even in the deepest forest you can sniff the salt
and follow it to the coast.

But the rules of this rough country are different.
Head out on a hunch in a straight path
(should that even be possible)
and a hiker could go a thousand miles

(if it is the wrong direction)
and never bump into a soul
or a trace of civilization.

So the lost hiker sits and thinks,
waiting for the funnel of blackflies
to descend on him from the heavens.
The raven keeps vigil
hoping perhaps to eventually
pick the gristle off my bones.

Then suddenly I am twelve again
and reading a book
about survival in the woods.
The protocol is clear.
When you are lost,
at first, stay put.
Make this your ground zero.
Then circle round your base
once, then twice,
then three times and beyond —
each time a wider orbit,
ever vigilant for some small shred of evidence
as to the way out.
But always return if need be
to centre ground
and keep your head
and listen to your heart
as you practice those ancient skills
of designing your own salvation
when no one else can save you.

Three Ways to Remember Winter

I

wavelap on snowtoast wintercrust
sunribbon razorblue skyrip sting of winter
oceanedge cityfeet shuffle saltsand
and gentlekick icesilver slivers of ice and rock
pebble and shell back to sea
from beachbreak bib of tide and time

II

gullrip sound of wing and beak
backing down the windwhip
fearstruck from inland man
wading gundeath on saltmarsh squadron
bulletready to retrieve light
from the eye of neverready skyswimmers

III

tidal water of seastilled level sand
salt sidewalk for city footslap
of boots that break and break and begin again
rubberfoot slap on sea and sand
easypaced miracle of manwalk
twofoot parade of mammal legs
lifeblood thump of saltblood seeker

Fog

Fog falling in on Halifax
leaning wet and windless against the legislature
feeling its way up through the sockets of the city
and emptying the spaces from emptiness
in a soft military parade of completion.

Fog sidling up against the dockyards
and thick and soft on the rat's back
with pearling globes of the sea.
We are with you, fog,
stalled high up in your forest on the bridge at night
over the harbour heaped with your awful soft foliage.
To jump tonight would be to dissolve slowly to sweat and salt
and rich pungent ferment
to never reach the concrete of
absolute harbour top
rhymeless tonight without wind
paved rutless by fog.

Fog feeling up the city
up Barrington up Prince up Blowers up Brunswick
up the pant leg of the rumhappy man
drinking too late to make his way to Hope Cottage
or the Salvation Army for sentimental soup and leftovers.

Fog — clean and grey and green and warm
and freezing and collecting like pollen
on nose hairs
burrowing into ears and
drilling out nail holes in tenements
kneeling outside the doors of widows
whose husbands sank beneath your perfect
embrace in your blind efforts at fulfillment.

Fog sucking out sewers of human perfume
scouring the sulfur from
the Power Corporation stacks

and slapping it down like brown chewing gum
on the hoods of rusting Hondas and hatchbacks
and half-ton pickups.
You won't leave us alone
a sinking sky beneath the unseen stars
reminding us of how close we cling to this planet
how easily we might drive stakes through our own hearts
or dream ourselves into holocausts
as we breathe your mix
of our own gashouse anaesthesia.

Where there is life on this coast
the fog will dance among the rocks
glazing the graffitti of boulders
at Black Rock Beach
or hounding with seaspit the monuments
to sunken navies and shattered empires.

Carl Sandburg you know nothing of fog
of intoxicating Halifax sea breath
lusting after the land
landlording the night
with mysterious inner light coming from nowhere
but everywhere
complete
consummate.

Fog cleaning the shoes of Winston Churchill
frozen in front of the public library,
fog borrowing alleys to sleep in trash cans
brimful with the hardware of our dreams,
fog the great constable of noise
on whose ear the throats of civilization go quiet.

We're with you fog
hiding out in the Public Gardens after dark
locked in between the massive Victorian swing gates
we're with you nibbling at the leaves of trees
planted by English kings and princesses

we're with you crawling out with the mice
from under the gazebo where the music
of two world wars screamed sour in the dawn
we're with you planning designs on the tulips
the roses, the rosaries left on the porch
by dozing nuns across Spring Garden Road.

Fog — in spring you speak forever death
in winter forever life
we believe in the weight of your sleep
your ageless supple spine
your painless powerful jaws
like shark's teeth muffled in angel wings.
For you we define the limits of soft.

We are with you here in Halifax
and linked to the kelp in your breath
tied to the strings of Sable
and tethered to the lip of the Great Shelf.
We can sing like this with the tongues of cod
the ribs of stone
and the bartered symphonies of barnacled whales.
We can trust the rivets of your silence
even here in the riddled city.

I hold your hand
stumbling through the potholes of Water Street.
You make me feel the pulse of my blood
like yours
salted and cool.

The Evaporation of Saints

So many are lost
in bright sun and wind and government.
I have met five in my life,
all are now dead as saints must be.
Each was brave enough
to disbelieve violence
to grow green life from bedrock
and to avoid taxes
for a while.

You never meet a happy saint.
They all suffer as they must
for all of us.
Through their grief
we are permitted to go on,
to do what we do best,
to conspire new methods
for destroying
the saint
in all of us.

Angus (Giant) MacAskill Smiles North from the Right Hemisphere of His Brain

Sometimes a man feels so small
from being so big
for so long.
You get tired of dreaming your life down to size
and hoping to wake up in a sensible bed
but it never happens.
When they took me to the States
I met women who fainted
as they tilted back to find my face,
but that's a world south of love
and big men were never built
for lopsided American passion.

Even home on Cape Breton
there was always a ruined man's money
on his palm daring me
to crack the chain links or hold back horses.
When you get old, the small man inside
wants you to unzip your spine
and let him out. He wants to
move around closer to earth
and, for once,
look straight into
other human eyes.

The Best Watermelon
Since the First World War

It was impossible for him to see
but he studied it with his hands,
thumping the side
with an eighty-six-year-old thumb
like he was tuning it up to play.

The big knife came down
on the cutting board
with that clean, hard sound
of cordwood being split
and he could tell from the smell
what state it had come from.

Nobody could spit seeds
like he did: a Gatling gun
aimed at a stainless steel sink
and there was religion in his chewing.
When he finished
he said,
"Take the rest of this
with you.
Don't leave any of it for me.
You're still young and can appreciate it.
You won't taste another one
like that,
not in this century
anyway."

Driving the Crow to Halifax

Wing dragging along the skirt of sea,
staring among the banquet guests
you waited for high tide and death
only to grow scared of living
when I found a washed-up net
and captured what remained of you.

Crowded into a box
you were amazed
at the craziness of death —
a hot trip to Halifax
in the backseat of a Pinto,
darkness and corrugated cardboard
all around like a dimwit purgatory.
Then came tape and wire cages
growing up around you, clamping off
the world and splicing metal against the light
while animals inside other lives
howled and scratched around you
in the linoleum nightmare
of this civilized, disinfected nowhere.

Back again through distance without motion,
without flight,
an understood death. There could be no life
without the wing, no breath without
air chasing down your lungs.
Past your beach, your cliff,
the kingdom once soldered fast
together by the parallel vision
of two dark eyes.

Two weeks later
you lose your stink of death,
eat dogfood
and bounce from perch to fence then back
like a manic downtown mercenary.

Your dreams fill up
with the feel of talons in dead things
still warm
on the highways of the imagination.
You cannot believe you are alive
and remain angry at whoever saved you.

If I'm not careful
you would unzip my chest with your claw,
snatch out my liver with your beak
and make me think twice
about the quality of mercy.

The Beach

Each seed of sand pulls vision down
until I lose the circus sky
that sings above my head.
I grow vast within each quartzite world
but cautious too and self-possessed
until applause from smashing waves
pulls me back
to the other plane
of distance
and possibility.

I come here often
to see the change of swell
and shift of tide
to mark advances and retreats.
This beach erases the inland ways
and sends me reeling
with mantras of saltwater
singing itself into nothing
on the sand.

The Melting

The icicle in the bathtub is crawling toward the drain.
I drink in its melting with my eyes
and inside my ears
play back the sound it made
as I snapped it from the soffit
taller than a man
and rigid with a spine
of cold, clean music trapped
in vivid silence.

When it broke free into my warm hand
it sang one perfect note
that made the sky ache blue
and long after the tone had sounded
I kept it going in the echo chamber
behind my throat
sustained like a chanting mirror
as I carried the bright tenor
in to my daughter
who wondered at the melting glass
in my blue knuckles.

She sang to it immediately,
instinct pulling music from her
as I stood it on end and she danced around it,
herself on every side
and each self rippled and revised.

And when the dog began to lap at the puddle on the floor
we took the ice to rest.
In the yellow tub, full length,
it wept its clear blood out
until we all had grown back
into our other selves
and something inside me began to fold
a blanket tight
around one cold and perfect digression.

The Headlands

The latent springsnap of ice and snow in Nova Scotia
thaws the corded ribbons of the wind,
the blue burning sea
sings through the river of nerves
and we are almost alive
unstuck in the crowded commons of the unnarrowing day
and flapping wings fine-tuned
to the cadence of the melting cantos.

East of Halifax
the stubborn but surrendered hills
feel the stony lap of melted cap ice
rattling among their rocky knees,
the headlands once nameless and inland
now barking with waves and human voices:
Devils Island, Hartlen Point, Osborne Head, Pennsy Head,
Egg Island, Lawrencetown Head, Sellars Head, Leslie Island
— all edited by the sea, left parenthetical
against the wind
as if somewhere on the other side in Brittany
or lost in the salvaged Azores
you could find the rest,
the completion of the geological event.
But no,
we are alone here with the Atlantic,
a high-booted mistress with an angry whip
and cold grey eyes that linger
outside bedrooms
for foggy months of sentencing.

And Newfoundland was once attached to Africa,
a long drift north and east to independence
then dependence crafted by well-intentioned governors
who weaned the spirit of selfhood
with the skin of wilted handshakes.
Here to the south we are thankful to that island

that blocks the pack ice
that bends the Labrador Current east
hurling it back toward Iceland,
England and the Scots
with bitter but unsustained revenge.
More courageous than we are those rockbound
icelocked harbourmen who, come spring,
must greet the sea
with dynamite
for a fair shake at her treasured womb.

But here the rocks bleed out their winter
and grow like wisdom teeth
on the shrinking skull of the hill
while today, Palm Sunday,
I fall back into myself and eulogize
the undoing of my innocence.

I have in my own way bent back the sky
and doubled up the steep sea
looking for an entrance to heaven
and safe passage away from the looming headlands
where flesh can only succeed
against all the gravities of the world
through pain and suffering.

Qualifying for Membership

On the ferry to Ceuta,
halfway between Spain and Morocco,
Europe and Africa,
my complacent past and my terrifying future,
I meet a man from Toronto
handcuffed to a briefcase
and leaning like a plank against the rail
while gulls swoop low against the bow.
I explain that I'm scared, I've
been gone 28 days,
already the vacuum I left
in North American lives is filling in.
Even as I sipped vodka on the Icelandic flight east
the wounds were healing
while I still contemplated
the dripping weapon of my exit.
And there would be more distance
accumulated like money across North Africa,
the Middle East, the impossible Asian miles,
as the vacuum in my wake would trail behind
like a threatening banner
to eventually become complete
as I arrive back home having
split the planet in two.

The man from Toronto listened patiently,
dangling his briefcase
over the foaming sea.
You're wrong, he told me.
The first month is the hardest,
after that you'll never want
to go home again.
The world will be a different place.
He'd been gone twenty years
and never once gone back.
I wanted to hear more

but we were snug in the harbour
and I lost him in the crowded exodus.
When I stalled in the lineup by the ramp
I grabbed the rail and held fast,
heard a stiff voice from behind
crack, "Keep moving"
in English.

Bodhisattvas Always Finish Last

Somewhere in the middle of Texas
beneath the interstate overpass
a fellow hitchhiker offers me
half a hero sandwich,
says we're all part of a chosen family —
wandering around a complicated continent
making circles out of straight lines
and living like Indians.
I'm cold and tired.
Just learning the trade,
he says, a shaman
offering me his onions
while explaining
his sister's miscarriage in Missouri,
his mother's divorce in Washington
and a man in California
who told him he could have
a free swimming pool
if he could take it with him.

He didn't even carry a pack, explaining
that a truck driver won't let you starve,
the earth will never deny you a bed
and the only way to be
free
is to empty your pockets

of everything but lint
and never allow the sun
to come up in the same place
twice.

My Grandmother's Father

Dragged his wife and my grandmother west
to earthquakes in San Francisco
and land rushes in Texas
always travelling by train
liking the feel of parallel tracks
sliding away beneath him across a continent.

The woman preferred Philadelphia
which was only west of New Jersey
and nowhere on the itinerary.

A good man, he never drank,
but was restless for new desert
and rock jacked up rigid at the sky
holding down jobs as a flapjack cook
or hotel clerk
until she hauled them back
to the ultimate Philadelphia
to save the marriage.

There he lost a leg to tuberculosis
and had to leave his wife,
limping to the docks to catch a freighter
for the long way around to the other coast
where a half-shattered heart and one good leg
couldn't support a panhandler
in a gold rush.

Encounter With an Immortal

He was alive, breathing, drinking a can of Coors
on the interstate in Connecticut
fastened behind the wheel of an old Ford van
abandoned by some Midwest phone company.

Picked us up hitchhiking,
said the floor might hold past Hartford,
that the valves were burnt to powdered crystal,
that he was alive, breathing, well
into his second case
and had spent the night alone with one headlight
on the Pennsy Turnpike dodging potholes and troopers.

Said the world was a helluva place
as long as you had half a tank of gas
and some beer,
asked if we ever read Kerouac —
On the Road. Did we remember
the kid who pissed off the back of the flatbed truck
tearing across Nowhere, Kansas?

Belched that it was him, the very man
behind this very steering wheel
alive, breathing, wondering
if we'd mind chipping in a dollar for gas.
Said he had a pair of beers left if we wanted them,
confessed that it wasn't always easy
being a legend, that it was hard
to keep up the pace
after 45.

Balloon Tires

Once they start paving, it's all over.
First you lose the pothole aquarium,
then they move the ecstasy of ditches underground
and seal them up in concrete tubes.
Sandy fields yield asphalt and bloom straight white lines,
diagrams for parking and living.
You wake up one morning and realize
a baseball field has been swallowed by Woolco
and second base is in Housewares.
You miss the smell of clean dirt
and the glue of mud on your fingers,
you wonder if your grandfather
could take some giant plow
and turn it under to rot
so everything could grow back.

Late on a warm, drizzled night
when the streetlights stage musicals
with the damp air
you climb on a black bicycle
and speed off
down a dark street
with soft new feminine pavement
and plunge downhill fast beyond confusion.
When the new neighbours see you upright,
arms folded, eyes closed,
sucked by giant magnets to the unfinished road,
they wonder what sort of place they have moved to,
they wonder if the town is safe.

The Wreck

The boiler's left and captain's bridge;
he lost her thirty years ago,
the sea grew teeth to chew through steel
and now the bank is littered sheaves
of iron planks and barbs of bolts
sheared down and whittled into bones
of bleeding rust as sharp as pain.

Once violence blends itself to shore,
all broken, useless half-lost things
find refuge here among the rocks,
grow brown with kelp
and red with dulse,
then mussels, Irish moss and snails.

The inlet here is thin and quick
two trimmed spruce sticks
mark fortune's door.
If fishermen from Rocky Run
want home before a setting sun
they have to cut the bargain close
with supper and a tide that slips
to growling rocks
and gruesome chores.

Factory Seconds

When my grandfather gave up the house,
he left behind a garage full
of cigar boxes, all factory seconds,
empty or crammed with different sized screws
that someday might have been put to use.

The house was bought by a career placement agency
and my grandfather had already remarried
a woman no one else in the family liked
because she was Catholic and lived
in a cottage on the Pennsauken Creek.

I was the last to sort out the pickings
before the church rummage sale organizers
and I thought of my grandmother, dead
a couple of years from some cancerous thing
the size of a grapefruit
and glad the old guy wouldn't have to sit
alone in the blue-green light
of the Niagara Falls lamp
smoking his cut-rate panatellas.

There was grandeur in those massive ladders
of brown boxes with the basic black labels
that coughed out the phrase
which sounded like Time's own warning
against the ticking of industrial employment.
Collecting a few empties, I hit upon
a box religiously crammed with love letters,
Gertrude to George, circa 1918.

They had apparently lived some miles apart.
She was the subject of her mother's warnings
while he was caught up in the muddy grip of global politics.
Unfurling one tightly coiled paper cylinder, brown
like old leaves, I read my grandmother's chastising
from so early on in the century:

"I love you very much, George, but hope you will learn
to give up those cigars as God would have you do."

In his own way, I suppose he compromised, buying only
the cheapest stogies money could buy and never
once hiding the evidence but piling it up like insulation
along the walls as he smoked and repaired
tractor transmissions from the grease pit in the floor,
while a non-smoking God turned a blind eye
on deeper bargains arranged between spirit and flesh.

Paterson

Finished teaching an English class
late one night in Paterson
and was locking up the door to the rented classroom
just above the tattoo parlour
when a crooked little man
drives an elbow in my spleen for my wallet.

I'm not dumb.
Here, take it —
eight bucks and a telephone dime.
He's high on something,
could be codeine
and you can tell he's hurtin'
with a bad back, all stooped over
and stoned in a sad way,
not even happy about having scored
without a fight.
I just stand there,
turn to go, who knows
knives maybe somewhere
inside all that pain
but then he stumbles over backwards
made smaller and sadder by the money
and all alone with a dead wallet.

He starts cursin' himself
then crashes butt first down a basement stairway
all agony and hard, brittle noises.
The world is wrapped tight like wire
around his throat, the scream
is plate glass in the night.
I broke my damn arm, he says,
I ain't no good
and this town ain't nothin'.
You gotta help me, man.

I wind his good arm around me,
lift him like a broken bicycle
wrapped in stinking meat.
I'm half inside his clothes
and it's like death in there. We're both scared
someone's watching.
Only thing worse than fear, he tells me,
is bein' alone
with all them bastards out there
watching.

On Becoming a Canadian Citizen

This month I become Canadian,
giving up on the tired, malignant love of America,
wanting the cold of a purifying north.
It's good to become a foreigner,
to pretend you are no longer what you were.
I'm giving up the arms race, the space race,
a chance to be a marine, an astronaut,
a president, a teller in the Chase Manhattan Bank,
a would-be assassin.

Physical changes will take place;
bones will grow back in hollow places
and my blood will turn a new colour.
The judge will ask my name and I will answer,
"Tundra," then sing anthems of geese,
track ice around the courthouse
and howl with my new-found Borealis.
All my friends will be there
helping me invent my new country
and sending postcards to the failed refugees south.

Someone will make me promise
to love an empire
stretched thin against an empty sky
but later, alone,
on a quiet hill,
the sea will question my politics,
the spruce will want more than professed loyalty
and the armies of the paranoid
will be short one soldier.

Lawrencetown River

Green fusion, dark in channels,
aches for something broad
but here the river carves the sand,
breeds mussel and crab
and anxious, almost visible swimmers
with lives forever aimed against the current.

A man could never starve here
but could go blind from morning beauty,
go deaf with the quiet
or lose himself beyond repair
in the delicacy of the wind.

Here, fresh water
heaves against the salt,
revises sand into erotic shapes,
with lusty hieroglyphs on the shoreline.
With the proper codebook
I could read these tracks
and other news
left by gulls and herons
at daybreak,
a silent time of light
and longing.

Remembering Summer

And now I'm stopped, I can't move on.
This was the place I tripped to sea
and fell into hostile pools,
stabbed by living blades of whelk and black mussel,
my bones battered by the rocks
until I learned to swim again,
slipping with the diminished current.

Before me I saw the sad, soft shape of a woman's back
as natural as if it belonged here, a creature of the sea —
no human face at first, no panicked cry or signature of fear.
But when turned skyward, the eyes were somewhere else,
some inner harbour, some safer place than this.

No breath, no whisper, no flush of pumping blood,
just cold of white and echoing blue,
the colours the sea would want upon a grave.
She was focused on some farther shore
but I could only turn and swim
back to the one that I knew best,
the waves now helping us in
as the river spent its power beyond the land.

As my feet found the first advancing rock,
I steadied myself,
began to breathe life back into my companion,
suddenly more intimate than any woman
I had ever kissed before.
With each shared breath, the empty eyes
and hollow cheeks seemed more familiar.
I told her I refused to quit
with each new painful breath,
but there was something that I tasted on those lips
unlike any others I had found.

She had no trace of fear;
I had collected it all for myself

and could not hide it as I pushed air into her lungs
suddenly wanting to escape, go home,
and savour the lips of the living.
Instead, blind, sweet terror led me on
as her eyes fixed on that empty sky
and her heart became another cold stone on
this cluttered coast.

When all had failed and a crowd had come,
still white with my first fight with death,
I climbed the cliff,
the hill grown cruel enough
to steal the muscles from my legs
and headed home,
the herons rising up from the marsh
as my throat grew tight
and I wished an end to summer everywhere,
a return to the cold comforts
of the empty shores of winter.

A Retreat to Tender Traps

Near the mouth of Rocky Run —
a fragile channel and a long spit of shaggy rock
still bar me from the open sea.
I feel inland and cheated,
too late for missed chances to ford the shallows
so it's back toward land
still needing first to catch the sting of icy streams
until I find I'm into muck beyond my knees
and reaching up with hungry gums.

I'm free at length and double back
around the snake, I'm barefoot now
and fighting for my space
on crowded floors of living shells with razored beaks.
Another try, it's quicksand now, of sorts,
and oh those happy clams
who sense me sinking in the soup —
an old relation coming home
but finally a place is found,
a plane of corrugated sand
and I discover my feet upon
God's own, uncharted clam bed,
untouched by all the diggers of this world.

But now the sky grows wild with living wind
and dancing birds who want this place;
I'm crowded now by dowitchers and siren snipes
all needle-nosed and locomotive-legged
who flutter at my advance
until I crawl way up, above the bar
to beachrock and glasswort
and an infinity of spider legs.

My hand moves to shuffle the stones
and write among these rocks
of all the miracles
just as a lone sparrow

attaches itself to a swaying stem of sea oats
beside my cheek.
The wind begins to dry my feet,
the sun pretends it was
and will forever be
like this eternal present
flashing phosphorus
on the landscape of empty history.

11:30 a.m., Three Fathom Harbour

Clam beds now — soft, footsucking mud
and vivid streamlets running south.
The harbour will be full up soon
to end decisions about where to walk.
I hope to beat the tide
and sprint
across a patio of slime
skinned over with a crust
of sun-fried eelgrass.

Speed, I decide, makes a lighter soul
so I charge across
only to find myself halfway
up to my crotch in silt
and staring down an awkward death,
mud already grabbing
at what's left of my manhood.

I heave my pack to higher ground
and lean as best I can,
to swim perhaps, or crawl or flail
as I watch my skin begin to turn
its way back into the ooze.

But one foot has found its freedom
even as it clings in communion
with who knows what
sort of worm in these depths.
In a fresh advance, I ascend from muck
evolve back to a man,
my gills closing tight as I nurse my pride
and rest beside
a tin cup with buckshot holes
cradling snails and snails
and more snails.

September 8: The Cove, Seaforth

The railroad is erasing itself.
All summer, men
with rust-stained skins
have undone ribs of steel
that linked this shore.
The owners want it all away —
the gypsum's gone for good.
These Seaforth rails will melt
then boil
and pour themselves in something else
until this spur
is everywhere but here
where wave roar and diesel thrust
once staged a volley of staggering noise.

Here at the cove old boxcars
once lingered a winter;
the freight men hoped they'd just disappear.
The sea and other vandals
would be a cheap wrecking crew
but never quite up to the conspiracy
of shaving six-inch steel
into blossoms of rust and thin air
in a single season.

In fifty years the rail has been and gone.
There's nothing left but me
on foot above the tide
collecting wasted bolts as red as dulse
and heavy as the anchors
of unwanted history.

Facing Rat Rock

The tide has sealed us off
from one farther island,
a low lump of stone
whose name seals its fate.
A gutted shack stands above the rockweed
and we think that would be a good place
to undo
whatever ties a man to civilization.

Clear pools grow red and golden fronds
and periwinkle shells make minarets along the shore
where a thousand snails have crawled
to issue up these bleached monuments
before drying up to death
beneath a helpful sun.

The sea does here
what must be done,
carving away at things that are hard,
stealing the soil and littering rocks,
then giving back new life
to glisten like jewelry
that sits out high tide before slipping home.

I ask my brother what things make him happy
but he doesn't know.
We share an affliction
with much of the world
and the more I pry
at what makes him tick,
the more we confound ourselves,
give up, leave the logic to the mounting wind
and screaming gulls.

High up on the Wedge Island top
we find a well —
the walls of the ridge drop off close on either side

but when we lift the cover
the water sits high;
it's fresh, not salt, and nearly spills above the lip.
With opportunity still alive
we close the lid
and leave the fount untasted.
There's something to be feared perhaps
from water trapped like this
and surrounded mostly by sky.
My brother is thinking of bacteria.
I'm wondering who tapped this hill and when
and what of the powers of something wet
that pushes up
from such dark stone depths?

One day soon, the sea will meet this well
and steal the rocks that once made walls
until it gushes free on every side
and spends itself at last
in salt.

Later,
I recognize what we've missed:
a chance to taste of something pure.
We've backed away from cliffs again
and scatter all the fledgling gulls
who make for flight
but fail to rise
as elder claws flash past our heads
and wings flap hard
like circus tents about to fall.

The Chanterelles, The Rage

A field creeps down to the edge
in wild aster and goldenrod,
a seduction of inland ways,
and I'm drawn up to the higher land
then pulled inside the woods
by colour on the needled floor.
Mushrooms — this year a bumper crop
from endless rains and cold
(our summer spent itself in two weeks,
a heartless thanks for surviving winter).

This duel I've staged with death is here again.
The glowing amanita I can trust, it's poison worn
like a harlequin shirt
but the chanterelles (their very name a song)
are dull gold gone ripe
and mostly safe but some are not.

A mushroom calls you down
beneath wet blue-green boughs
to judge the dark regimes.
The forest draws me further in
then sets me down to teach me this:
false chanterelle (the poison one)
has blades for gills beneath the cap;
the real one's blunt and small
and underneath, the ridges bridge
like nerves or veins inside your wrist.

April Iceberg Off Bragg's Island

from a print by David Blackwood

The hand of God has hacked this ship
from eaves of ice that roof the world
and now it floats in silent strength
reminding me of the cold, blind force
that shapes our lives and feeds our fears.

We row at night in boats to feel
the new blue light of moon and ice
beneath this cold and ancient dream
that wants to test our own beliefs.
It almost seems like holiness
to stand this small beneath these cliffs,
these vaulted walls of winter white.

You feel the weight deep down inside
like thunder or extinction's calm.
Had I the heart
I'd climb the sides
to meet the moon
and leave a harsh and ragged land
to float off south to other seas
till nothing's left but warmth
and waves.

Beautiful Sadness

I was always afraid of Beautiful Sadness
because I believed she was friends with despair and misery
but now, driving on the empty Halifax street
I realize I want to know Beautiful Sadness.
I'm only driving a small Czechoslovakian car
but I want to stop and open all the doors
to the beautifully lost.
I want to drive them anywhere they want to go
because someday
I know I'll be one of them
and I want to know what it's like.

Now Beautiful Sadness is private and quiet
with her suffering
and wants me to sit through endless stoplights
cataloguing all the irretrievable past —
blue childhood, bright innocence,
each vivid gash of love
until it fades to dull ash and washes into the earth.
Then Beautiful Sadness comes along
and tugs at the memory that insists
the road ahead is not enough;
there are other highways back to powerful emotion.

So I'll pull off onto a slushy side street
and dream a song to you, Beautiful Sadness,
until warm regret fuels the traffic in my head
sends me back into the stream of grey hope and urgency.
But first, I'll say, I love you Beautiful Sadness.
Stay close and melt my ambition.
The strength of your weakness must grow
inside the garden of my heart
to give soft power to the ache that drives me home,
even as I attempt escape.

We've Reached the Age

We've reached the age
when eyes reverse the dream and dare
to see the sense of subtle things
beneath this shell of innocence.

This winter's cold
another stage
for frozen sap and sleepless nights
while summer's light
buys better moods,
another wider, healthy ring
beneath this bark,
this crust, this skin.

Let stronger breath draw ice from veins
and melt the panic from our limbs
like chainsaws tuned to terror's touch,
a candle's flame might char the sun.
Our lifeblood dries at length and sets
within the grain like ancient art.
When wedges pry so deep within
our spirit cracks the cold and sings.

The Truth

It used to be
The Truth was always teasing me,
sending me flyers in the mail,
lying in wait in snowdrifts
or calling to me from empty classrooms.
In fact, The Truth was always
distracting me from what I was doing;
it wanted my attention
or wanted me for an audience.
I never knew what to do but follow it
or listen to it sing.

Some days when I'm happy now
The Truth is hungry for revenge
and I feel like somebody with a car radio
pushing buttons all the time,
wanting to hear all the stations at once.

The Truth is all around, I suppose,
but it's not the same,
not like the old days,
when The Truth paraded up and down the streets
and wore a name tag
just in case you got confused.
Lately, though, The Truth stays inside.
It spends a lot of time on the phone.
I think The Truth is into sales and real estate
and mutual funds.
The Truth is at home with the financial pages
and sports section and obituaries;
it has an answering machine
so it doesn't miss any important phone calls.

I'm afraid The Truth forgets
what it was like to be young,
to be confused, to be afraid.

Confidence is something The Truth likes to brag about.
This worries me a lot.
I'm not sure
I want to hang out with The Truth
anymore
because maybe
The Truth is just learning how to lie,
or maybe it's been lying all along.

Cold/Winter

Six a.m. kitchen window: frost streaked like
a roadmap of the Midwest, highways always
crossing at rigid angles.
Thermometer visible: paint missing from numbers,
a string of breathless zeros,
red mercury curled up like a winter fox.
Wind moves the tire swing: ice lies snug in the bottom,
a vagrant rider,
the unborn icy soul of a child.
Splitting wood for the stove: I find long, thin crystals,
ice wedged between the grain,
surprising me like tiny, silver daggers.
Inside, near the fire: fruit flies come alive,
an accident,
they fly toward the platinum light of the window,
looking for spring
but then, at the sudden drop of temperature,
forget they are alive.

First Day of Duck Hunting Season
October 20, 2012

The shots ring out at first light
after a dark night of the season's first frost.
Beyond my withered garden
the hunter lies in wait
and I sadly muse
that some things you just can't change.

All summer the safety
of birds on water
was enshrined in those
warm liquid days
but now this.

A man from the city,
a harbinger of death,
parks his black truck
by the paved road
and wades the salty, still pools
before the moon has set.
He crouches low behind a bush
and loads his gun
and waits.

I know, I know.
It's not my land.
I have no right.
But still, at sixty,
having failed to fix the world,
having lived to see all that I have seen,
I wish to augment
the many miracles of my life
with at least one more.
So I speak a silent prayer
for all the morning ducks
to lift now from this cool October lake

into the sweet salt air
and venture off
in silence,
unbroken by the punctuation
of gunfire.

The Age-Old Question

Yes, it's still not clear.
The critics still debate,
was Giuseppe Arcimboldo,
the sixteenth-century Italian painter,
fully deranged
or was he a whimsical genius?
His fruity portraits,
his vegetable heads,
speak volumes of who we are
and how we should laugh
at our own pretense
of being masters of this world
when our true definition is thus:
organic molecules collected together
in these lovely sacks of skin
for this short and frenzied dance
in a green and splendid garden
delicately created
by the not-so-subtle
brushstrokes
of a god we hardly know.

Traction

Hands on the rim of all possibility, I'm haunted home
barricaded on four sides by darkness
while up above the universe, unhinged,
dazzles me like a rowdy all-night service station
with check-the-oil slingshot eyes
and how's-the-air-in-the-tire politeness.
I know this feeling,
I know this comfortable bucket seat of longing
because I've been harnessed here before, heading home,
pistons lighting up underneath the hood like nova stars
burning tips off spark plugs
down inside the throat of my ambition.

This night, as always, speaks of dreams to me
dreams shiny as baby moon hubcaps twirling in the dawn,
dreams hot as the steaming manifold
of all my transgressions,
transmission dreams of lots of room in the passing lane.
But I have seen the night vandals
sliding up out of the automotive shadows.
Some spoke in vowels of exhaust and drank 40-weight oil;
some could be here right now
ready to jimmy the lock on the door,
ready to undo the lug nuts of my highest hopes
or drain acid from the battery of my will
then spit it into my face until I go blind.

But my car tells me it's not like that at all.
It's pure, lubricated heart tells me I am part of the plan,
I'm in control, hands gripping the wheel
in karmic coincidence double-white-line inevitability.
Count the headlights on the highway —
all the high beam hopes, the low beams shutter
just as you spring free
from the grip of reason around a corner
and find you're staring into the raging sun
of some other five-speed god

who's saving suicide for the safety of the final thrill.
But no victims please, just the long trip home where
up ahead you'll find the long dark tunnel
your only guide the radio
who sings to you like a quadraphonic cowgirl in the sand
as I navigate through the potholes of evolution.
While the backseat hitchhikers
fall asleep like philosophical dust
and the ghosts of tomorrow crawl into the trunk
to sleep it off,
I steer clear of disaster, shovel darkness behind me
and burn on into the blistering night
until my tires sing that driveway song of home.

Now I see the needle pointing toward E
like a desperate junkie.
But I've been here before, I know that all I have to do
is tap a vein and siphon blood
straight into the roaring heart of my machine
and pop the clutch on reality altogether,
set the heater on high,
somewhere past infinity.
No Mountie this side of Mars can stop me now.
Once the highway slides past stony clouds and ozone trails
the heart begins to work like a self-serve no-lead pump
the only one for a million miles inside this desert of amnesia.

The Ladder

February 27, 2007

The cadence of winter had left
brown earth and scud ice beyond the fence.
The pheasants on this morning were waiting for me
to toss cracked corn on the frosted grass,
the old hen, brown as an old shoe,
walking right up to me now.
The old girl, she trusted me,
while her suspicious sisters hovered in the tall, stiff weeds.
Morning was a time of sighing and dismay,
feeling sorrow for every snowflake, every stationary star.
I tried to rid the world of murder, fraud and greed
but failed by noon like all the rest,
the wind stealing the important words from me,
stripping them of meaning
and tossing their husks back into my face.

A new mirror in the house showed a different me;
the photo in the paper looked less and less like the boy
my mother raised.
The mind is a delicate toy
that echoes with old passions
and new ones,
like dreams on a dirty floor
or dust and cold coffee.
And then a visit from an imagined angel,
the mute one who shows up
when a man is in his fifties
and she just stands there
watching.

There are planes leaving for India this morning
and the passengers discuss my absence.
But the rest of the world
believes I am working,
conjuring cures for heartbreak

charting old wounds
faking the words to an old Bob Dylan tune
or washing laundry and hanging it to freeze
by the healthy spruce trees.

Outside, the ground is hard, frozen, indifferent.
At its very least, this is a cold, adequate life
but that is the passive version.
There is fire at the foot of the ladder
and I am climbing it rung by rung
into the calm heavens,
the way old men disappear into dreams.

And Suddenly I'm Happy

Wake up late and feel forgotten,
breakfast alone with milk and granola.
The sun is out, a million things to do,
the world fills up with reason
and schedule
but I'm home by myself —
sitting before a window
that frames the wide marsh,
the sea.
Five thousand starlings line up on the wire,
a light puff of north wind
and they become a single silver wing.
I try to begin some honest work
here at my old desk
but wander off
to smile at the trees.
I stand there for a minute
confused
and suddenly realize
I am happy
for no clear reason
at all.

Many of the poems in this book were originally published in the following books written by Lesley Choyce:

Re-inventing the Wheel. Fredericton: Fiddlehead Poetry Books, 1980.
"Cold/Winter," "Paint-By-Number Garden Of Gethsemane," "The Possible Ear of God," "Tom Gilbert's Pants," "40-Watt Lighthouse."

Fast Living. Fredericton: Fiddlehead Poetry Books, 1982.
"Modern Translations," "The Bill Tawger School of Etiquette," "Surfing Before the Hurricane," "Three Ways to Remember Winter."

The End of Ice. Fredericton: Goose Lane Editions, 1985.
"Fog," "Angus (Giant) MacAskill Smiles North from the Right Hemisphere of His Brain," "The Best Watermelon Since the First World War," "Driving the Crow to Halifax," "The Melting," "The Headlands," "The Evaporation of Saints."

The Top of the Heart. Saskatoon: Thistledown Press, 1986.
"Qualifying for Membership," "Bodhisattvas Always Finish Last," "Encounter With an Immortal," "My Grandmother's Father," "Balloon Tires," "Factory Seconds," "Paterson," "On Becoming a Canadian Citizen."

The Coastline of Forgetting. E. Lawrencetown: Pottersfield Press, 1995.
"Lawrencetown River," "Remembering Summer," "The Beach," "The Wreck," "A Retreat to Tender Traps," "11:30 a.m., Three Fathom Harbour," "Facing Rat Rock," "September 8: The Cove, Seaforth," "The Chanterelles, The Rage."

Beautiful Sadness. Victoria: Ekstasis Editions, 1998.
"I'm Alive. I Believe in Everything.," "Legend," "My Father, Shaking Pepper," "Saskatoon Bus Depot: 8 a.m. Sunday," "Best Minds," "This Poem," "The Man Who Borrowed the Bay of Fundy," "The White Wheelbarrow," "The Beautiful Thing About My Outhouse," "April Iceberg Off Bragg's Island," "Beautiful Sadness," "We've Reached the Age," "The Truth," "Traction," "And Suddenly I'm Happy."

Caution to the Wind. Victoria: Ekstasis Editions, 2000.
"My Daughter, With Knots," "Medicine Walk," "Blue Beach," "Black Locusts," "Trepidation," "The Necropolis, Glasgow," "Testament," "The Death of Donut Land and Other News," "A Love of Old Things," "Song of Myself," "Orion Keeps Me Honest."

Revenge of the Optimist. Victoria: Ekstasis Editions, 2004.
"All the Water in the World," "Writing Down the Wind," "Hauling Seaweed for My Garden," "This Poem is the Room," "Report from the Republic of Morning," "The Sophistication of Pencils," "Poem for Leander's Garage," "Driving North With the Dalai Lama," "The Language of Broken Things."

The Discipline of Ice. Victoria: Ekstasis Editions, 2009.
"The Discipline of Ice."

As True As I'm Sittin' Here
200 CAPE BRETON STORIES
edited by Brian Sutcliffe & Ronald Caplan

COLLECTED BY ARCHIE NEIL CHISHOLM—laughs, comebacks, ghosts, fairies, put-downs, and all-round wit—from Dan Angus Beaton, Jim St. Clair, Sid Timmons, Hector Doink MacDonald, Annie the Tailor MacPhee, and many more.

Stories that shorten the road, lighten the work, and fill the pauses between tunes, throughout Cape Breton Island.

220 PAGES • $17.95 • ISBN 1-895415-58-6

The Cabot Trail in Black & White
VOICES & PHOTOS FROM NORTHERN CAPE BRETON
by Ronald Caplan

A FASCINATING AND TRIUMPHANT BOOK, filled with much laughter, community life, and down-to-earth daily work. Here are 40 chapters and 150 photos about the Cabot Trail and its people. From over 25 years of *Cape Breton's Magazine*.

144 PAGES • $19.95 • ISBN 1-895415-99-3

The Stud Horse Boy
MEMOIRS OF A HORSE BREEDER'S SON
by Darryll Taylor

FROM HIS ROOTS in the horse breeding world of rural Nova Scotia, Darryll Taylor carries the reader through a young man's amazing storied day with great good humour, shocking but realistic scenes, and a passionate respect for the dying art of breeding horses and the lovely countryside in which it all takes place.

144 PAGES • $14.95 • ISBN 978-1-926908-11-3

White Eyes
16 STORIES
by LARRY GIBBONS

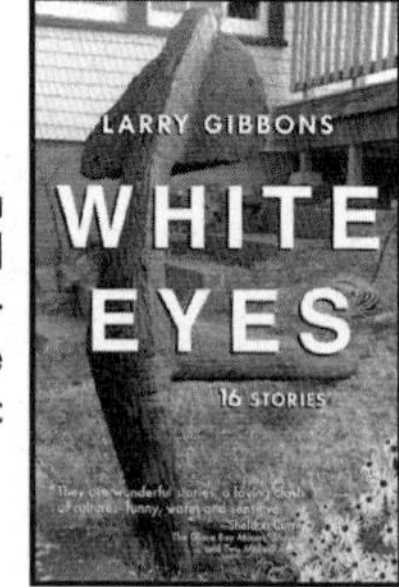

WELCOME TO THE WORLD of Larry Gibbons. Brought to a Mi'kmaw First Nation reserve by a woman's love, and privileged to live there for ten years, Gibbons has written a rare and extraordinary batch of short stories. Sometimes he gets it right. Often he is the confused white man. But story by story, he delivers terrific reading—compassionate, often comic and absolutely unique.

176 PAGES • $17.95 • ISBN 978-1-926908-07-6

Breton Books
Wreck Cove, Cape Breton, Nova Scotia B0C 1H0
bretonbooks@ns.sympatico.ca • 1-800-565-5140
www.capebretonbooks.com